When Someone You Love Is Dying

Some Thoughts to Help You Through

by Susanne Severeid

Photography by Pablo van Renterghem

SEVEREID COMMUNICATIONS • ASHLAND, OREGON

When Someone You Love Is Dying: Some Thoughts to Help You Through
by Susanne Severeid

Severeid Communications, Ashland, Oregon, U.S.A.
www.severeidcommunications.com

Concept and text by Susanne Severeid.

Cover and interior photographs by Pablo van Renterghem,
copyright © 2007-2016. All rights reserved.

To order photographs from any pages of this book, please visit:
www.pablovanphotography.com

Thanks to Chris Molé of Book Savvy Studio for her assistance in
publishing this book.

Printed in the United States of America

ISBN: 978-0-9909528-0-0

First Edition
Printed in the U.S.A.

To Tony,
Loving husband & father

"*Simple and beautiful. A most comprehensive book, When Someone You Love is Dying contains all of the information necessary to ease and comfort a loved one at the end of life. A first of its kind and a much-needed book.*"

E. Berman, caregiver, Oregon

This book is intended for those who are facing the possibility of death of someone they love. I have written it from the heart as a collection of thoughts and ideas in the simple hope that it might be of help to you, and to the one you love, during this most sad, stressful, and heart-wrenching time.

Having watched my beloved husband die, there are many things here that I did; there are some that I wish I had done, or had thought of. And so, I offer this to you,

> . . . from my heart to yours,
> *Susanne*

Uncertainty...
becomes the new name of the game. A diagnosis,
illness or tragic event can turn your world
upside-down. The future feels very frightening;
there is nothing concrete. There are no answers
or guarantees anymore.

... And, suddenly, you are tumbling down the
rabbit hole with nothing to hold onto.

But you do have something to hold onto.
The person you love is still with you.
You have the memories you have shared,
   the life you have had together,
      and the love you have for each other.

The person who is ill might be feeling lonely or afraid. Let them tell you what they are feeling. It will comfort them and make them feel less isolated.

Ask them...
>What do you want?
>>Where does it hurt?
>>>Is there anything I can do for you?

You might feel like
it's just the two of you
against the world.

Hold hands.

Be there.

Be present.

Put away your watch for awhile and just BE with the person. Focus on them, not on the long list of things you still have to do.

Remember to breathe.

Take deep breaths and try to find your center.

Find and hold onto your own calm place,

deep inside.

Speak of the old times and of memories shared. Let them talk about their childhood and their precious times.

If they want, bring out old photo albums and listen to their stories . . . even if you've heard them a hundred times before.

This is a season of your lives together. It has its own colors, its own rhythms. The pain is also a way to communicate on a deeper level, a way to get closer.

Be brave, be strong, and let it speak to you in its own way.

Patience. They are trying their best.
You are trying your best.
And it is very, very hard.

If they are sleepy or tired, let them rest.

Talk about the trips you've made
and the good times you've had.

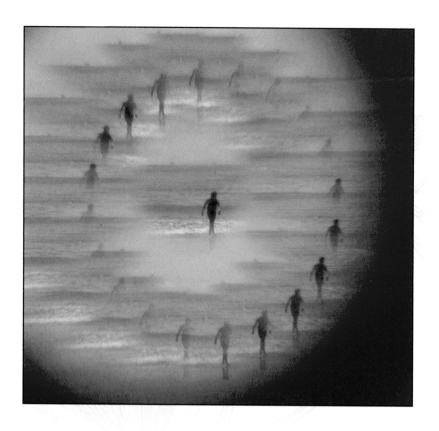

Remember when they were healthy and
happy and were not in pain or suffering.
Remember them as the <u>whole</u> person they
were ... and still are.

Let them talk about dying if they want to. If you can't be there for them in this way, then find someone else who can. It is important for them to be able to be honest about their feelings and their needs. Respect and support their choices and wishes.

Clear away the medical things, bring out a tablecloth, cloth napkins, and set a vase with fresh flowers from the garden on the table . . . even if it's only on the tray next to their bed.

Forgive them for everything...
if you can. If you do, tell them
that you forgive them.

Then . . . let them forgive you.

And then, do the hardest thing of all:
forgive yourself . . .
for any faults or shortcomings you
have had during this relationship.

Forgive yourself

. . . for being human.

Write them a letter thanking them for
all the things you are grateful to them for:
Things they have done for you.
Things they have done for others.
Things they have taught you.
The love they have given you.

Then, read it to them aloud.

In the same way that we enjoy the morning song of a tiny bird, savor the small moments you have together during this time.
Delight in the bliss and do not ask for any more than we ask of that little bird.

Ask them if they want to write down or record a message for anyone. If they don't want to, that's okay, too. Is there anyone, family or friends, that they want to see, be visited by, or call on the phone? If possible, help make this happen.

Contact is important and comforting in ways only the heart can understand.

If they are in a wheelchair, kneel or sit next to them so they can see your face.

And remember that if they can't get up to give you a hug, you can offer them one. If they can't come to you, go to them.

Help them make sure their paperwork is in order. It gives great peace of mind to all concerned to know that this is done.

Get support. Ask a good friend, an understanding family member, hospice nurse or clergy to help you and your loved one through this.

To just sit with you, to be a bridge, and to help you cope with the sadness and confused feelings.

Tell them how much they mean to you.
Tell them how much you will miss them.

Let the person be honest about their feelings; do not feel the need to change them or judge them. They have the right to their feelings, even if it might make you uncomfortable. Sometimes, people who are dying know better than the professionals treating them the truth about what is going on, and they have a right to their own truth.

Speak softly.

Plump their pillow.

Smooth their blanket.

Stroke their face gently.

Now is the time to cherish what you have
had together . . . and the time you still have
together.

While you both still can.

Be aware of the beauty that still
surrounds you . . . the look in their eyes,
the touch of their skin, the simple fact
that they are here with you, and that you
are here with them. Give each other as
much comfort as you possibly can.

And most of all . . .

   tell them that you love them . . .

      very, very much.

In grateful acknowledgement to all those who helped with this book.

The Mother and Son Team Behind
When Someone You Love Is Dying

Susanne Severeid is an award-winning author and performer whose writing (nonfiction and fiction) has appeared in book form, as well as in numerous newspapers and magazines. She also has an extensive background in radio and television.

Co-host/producer of the radio show, *Courageous Grief Talk*, KSKQ 89.5FM, with Julie Lockhart, Susanne is also a columnist for the *Ashland Daily Tidings* ("Mocha Musings"). She wrote *When Someone You Love Is Dying* after the death of her husband of many years in the hope that it will give comfort and be of help to others in similar situations.

www.susannesevereid.com

Pablo van Renterghem, Susanne's son, began taking photographs at the age of eight and has won several awards for his work. Twelve years old at the time of his father's death, Pablo has said that being able to express himself through the lens of a camera helped him to deal with his grief. "I have come to realize that life is very precious and not to be ignored. I love capturing life through a lens." He is currently attending university.

www.pablovanphotography.com

Made in the
USA
Middletown, DE